Stallions:
Their Management and Handling

NEIL DOUGALL

STALLIONS
Their Management and Handling

J. A. ALLEN & CO. LTD.
1 Lower Grosvenor Place
London SW1W 0EL

First Published in Great Britain by
J. A. ALLEN & CO. LTD.
1 Lower Grosvenor Place
London SW1W 0EL

© *1973 by Neil Dougall*

SBN 85131 256 x

First Published in this
edition 1973

Reprinted 1976

Reprinted 1983

Reprinted 1995

Printed in Hong Kong

For Regine

Acknowledgements

I wish to thank Mr. W. O. Case, Editor of "Horse and Hound", for permission to reproduce the material that appeared in the article "Way to Success in Stallion Management" in the March 19, 1971, issue of "Horse and Hound"; Captain E. Hartley Edwards, M.C., Editor of "Riding", for permission to reproduce parts of the article about stallion management which appeared in the March, 1972, issue of "Riding"; and "The British Racehorse" for permission to reproduce sections of the article "The Several Ways to Stallion Fitness" in the 1972 December Sales issue of that magazine.

I also wish to express my gratitude to all those stallion owners who provided pictures of their horses to illustrate this book, and to Mr. Peter D. Rossdale, M.A., F.R.C.V.S., for his photographs of mares being tried.

Contents

Spermatozoa — Fertilisation — When the Ovum is Not
Fertilised — Oestrus — When to Cover — Exceptions and
Variations.

General Principles — Trying Boards — Use of Gate or Fence
for Trying — The Natural Way — The Teaser — Methods of
Trying — On Thoroughbred Studs — On Other Studs —
Accurate Records of Trying — Frequency of Trying — On
Thoroughbred Studs — On Other Studs — The Shy Mare —
The Jealous, Bossy Mare — Prolonged Oestrus — Absence of
Oestrus — Foal Heat — Covering at the Foal Heat.

General Principles — Treatment After Service — Examination
for Abrasions — The Lungeing Stallion — The Stallion that
Bites — The "Slow" Stallion — Difficult Mares — Maiden
Mares — Specifics of Service — On Thoroughbred Studs — On
Other Studs — The Stallion's Book — Frequency of Covering.

Habits Which Last a Lifetime — First Turning-Out — Letting
Down Process — Trying Several Mares First — The First
Service — When the Stallion is not Successful — A Good Plan
— After the First Mare: One of Two Routes — The Best
Possible Base.

Illustrations

I
Friends

State of Mind — Two Factors Basic to Happiness — Relationship Between Stallion and Handler — Trust, Respect and Consistently Sympathetic Handling — Reprimand and Reward — The Bad-Tempered Stallion — Mutual Esteem.

Keep your stallion happy, healthy and fit, and you will be well on the way to success in his management.

A stallion's state of mind is of the utmost importance, since a happy horse will be much easier to work with and will make the most of his environment. And this in turn will have a very salutory effect upon his fertility. Up to a point, of course, a stallion's feeling of well-being depends upon the state of his health and his degree of fitness. But for the stallion that is not ranging free with his band of mares there are two factors which are basic to his happiness: the way in which he is kept; and his relationship with the person who handles him.

Try to treat your stallion as much like any other horse as you can. The better you succeed in doing this, within the limits imposed by the fact that he *is* a stallion, the happier he will be. Ideally, a stallion should run with a mare or two during the time he spends at grass. Once he has settled them they will supply him with all the equine company that he craves, and, provided they are quiet, good-tempered mares, they should not upset him in any way.

However, if your stallion is a valuable one you may not want to take the risk of letting him run with any other animal. In that case you should take extra care to allow him to indulge his natural gregariousness as much as possible, letting him see at least one other horse from his box, and, if he is a fairly sensible type, from his paddock too.

The worst way in which you can keep a stallion is to cage him up as if he were some sort of savage beast, confining him to a dark box or a high-fenced, close-boarded stallion pen so that he never sees another animal except at covering time. Such treatment can soon turn a stallion sour, and in the long run may make him dangerously ill-tempered.

A harmonious relationship between a stallion and the person who handles him is fundamental to the horse's happiness. At its best it is one of the most subtle and most satisfying relationships which can be developed between man and horse: here you have a large, powerful, proud and potentially dangerous animal, which, once you have established a basis of trust and respect and backed it up with consistently sympathetic handling, can become a true, and sometimes even affectionate, friend.

This particularly applies to the stallion that spends all his time on his own except for the relatively brief interludes of trying and covering. Such a horse will often become very dependent on his handler: he will enjoy your attentions, large or small, and will look forward to being taken out to exercise. And every so often he will greet you with that special nicker guaranteed to warm the heart of any horseman.

A stallion's trust in you is founded on his recognition that you genuinely like him, that you take care of him, and that you are consistently fair in your treatment of him; his respect upon the knowledge that you have no fear of him and that you will correct him promptly and adequately whenever he deserves it. It is absolutely vital that you should never show any fear of your stallion. If you are afraid of him he will soon sense it; then he will offer you neither trust nor respect.

However, to say that you should have no fear of your horse is not to suggest that you should ever take any liberties with him or be careless when you are around him. A healthy, well-fed stallion is always an active, virile and high-couraged animal, and even the best-tempered entire will have his off days when he is in a bad mood.

So you must always be alert and attentive, and properly tuned in to him. Be quietly confident, friendly but firm, patient and understanding, but do not make the mistake of ever taking him lightly or of handling him without the respect due to a large, powerful, serving male animal. Never put yourself in a position where the stallion can take advantage of you should he suddenly become so inclined, or where he can possibly hurt you.

A stallion can injure you easily enough, too, without meaning to do so. This can happen when he reacts instinctively to some powerful external stimulus and catches you unawares! He may suddenly become excited, as stallions will for all sorts of good reasons, and whirl, rear or plunge. If you are not wide-awake and ready when this happens, you may be cannoned into heavily, stamped on or dragged. You must stay one step ahead of a stallion mentally all the time, and, in fact, it is necessary to develop almost a sixth sense in this regard. Which is why anyone who contemplates handling an entire should already have a very good grounding in the care and control of other horses before he takes charge of the most high-couraged, most demanding equine of all.

By sympathetic handling I do not mean soft handling. From time to time your stallion will have to be reprimanded, the severity of the correction depending on just how far he has stepped out of line. Not to admonish a horse when he does something naughty or potentially dangerous is to do a great disservice to both him and you. Correction does not have to be severe (many times it may consist of nothing harsher than a sharply-spoken reproof) but it must register, it must be prompt and it must be consistent.

By the same token, reward him when he deserves it, but without sentimentality, which a stallion certainly will not appreciate. A stallion can be a true and generous friend, but never a pet.

What your relationship with the normal high-spirited but basically kind stallion should *never* be is that of a person attempting to bully a proud and noble animal into submission. Such treatment, involving the frequent and unnecessary use of stick or whip, severe bitting arrangements, much shouting and a complete lack of trust between horse and man, can only end in an unhappy, bitter and probably vengeful stallion.

Firmer-than-usual methods of handling will probably have to be employed, though, with the bad-tempered or vindictive stallion, an animal which may be really dangerous unless he is handled with resolution, and real skill and understanding. Occasionally you may even have to be quite harsh with such a horse, although never cruel or vengeful. A stallion of this type, whose temper may have been ruined by previous handling, or which may, especially if he is a Thoroughbred, have inherited a temperamental, irascible nature, is certainly no animal for a beginning stallion handler. He should be left to the man with years of experience.

Fortunately, such entires are not often encountered nowadays, although from time to time one does meet up with the older horse whose temper has been ruined by injudicious treatment, the young horse that has never been disciplined correctly, and the highly-bred horse that is unbalanced temperamentally.

However, I have found that no matter how kind and good-natured a stallion may be, any entire horse of spirit will try to get his own way from time to time. Such behaviour is an essential part of his proud personality, one fundamental facet of his natural role of leader of the herd, and you really would not want him to be any different. Nevertheless, you cannot afford to let him get away with it, since it is essential for you to nip potentially bad habits and potential disrespect in the bud. One of the foundations of true friendship between a stallion and his handler is certainly mutual esteem.

II
Healthy and Fit

Nutrition — Water — Necessity for Cleanliness — Exercise — Hard-Fit for the Breeding Season — Fairly Fit During the Rest of the Year — Grooming — Stabling — Worming and Vaccination — Hoof Care — Teeth.

You should make every effort to maintain your stallion in the best of health and to have him in hard muscular condition, without a trace of superfluous fat, for the covering season, and reasonably fit during the rest of the year. This is achieved by the skilful blending of food and water and exercise, by grooming and the provision of suitable stabling for the horse that is kept up, and by regular attention to worming, vaccination, feet and teeth.

The stallion must get enough of the right sort of food to satisfy his daily needs for energy and protein, minerals and vitamins. And given the tremendous influence that nutrition has upon a stallion's health, condition and fertility, the stallion feeder will need to have a really sound knowledge of the basic feed requirements of horses, backed up with much practical experience and a sharp eye for condition. In the final analysis, with horse feeding being so much more a matter of acute observation and skilled judgement than scientific measurement, it will certainly be the eye of the master that conditions the stallion.

Since a stallion's diet can range all the way from pasture alone to a combination of half-a-dozen or more feedingstuffs, it is obvious that no absolute rules can be laid down about feeding. The important thing is to provide the stallion with such a broad spectrum of nutrients that the possibility of him suffering from a deficiency of any sort is virtually ruled out. For instance, a good example of a satisfactory combination of feedingstuffs for stabled stallions is that which a Thoroughbred stallion kept up all year round might receive: lightly-crushed oats, broad bran, ryegrass-clover seeds hay, rock salt in the manger, a vitamin-mineral supplement, linseed mash once or twice a week, and pasture and/or freshly-cut green feed when available. While a horse is kept up, incidentally, his daily ration should be divided into at least three feeds.

Fresh, clean water should be available to the stallion at all times. If he is living out this means that he should always have access to a suitable stream, dam or trough. The stabled horse that spends a certain amount of time at grass every day should be provided with a supply of water in both box and paddock unless his box opens directly into the paddock and the box door is left open while he is outside.

Feed and water containers must be kept clean. You should make the cleaning of them a regular drill, daily for those in a stallion's box, because he has such an acute sense of smell that clean, sweet-smelling receptacles can play a big part in maintaining a keen edge to his appetite. Dirty, foul-smelling ones can have just the opposite effect, and also provide an ideal environment for germs.

Plenty of exercise is absolutely vital to the health, fitness and fertility of any stallion. Nature designed the stallion to be a tough, fit battler, always ready to protect his band of mares and foals from danger, particularly from predators, and forever prepared to fight off any other stallion that might try to take his mares away. He and his band roamed over large areas of land seeking out their food and water, and this constant, often demanding, physical exertion meant that the wild stallion was in hard muscular condition all year long. The high fertility of such stallions is legendary.

Now, given the artificial conditions under which so many stallions of all breeds live today, it is not necessary to have a horse as hard fit as his wild counterpart *except during the breeding season*. For that period of the year he must be produced as hard-muscled, as sound of wind and limb and as full of energy and enthusiasm as he would be under natural conditions, thus enabling him to function at his peak of fertility.

During the rest of the year he should be maintained in fairly fit condition, and it is unwise to allow a horse to slacken off completely once the breeding season is over and become soft and flabby. This is totally unnatural for any stallion. It also means that the annual preparation of the horse for the covering season, the business of getting him into really hard muscular condition, will be a much longer and much more demanding task than it would have been if he had been kept reasonably fit all the time.

There is also a certain amount of risk to the horse involved in getting a soft, flabby stallion into condition for covering, particularly if he is the excitable type. He is much more liable than is the reasonably fit horse to injure muscles, tendons and ligaments if he overdoes any part of the conditioning process, whether by making a sudden, unexpected about-face on the lunge or by being worked too fast, too hard or for too long by his handler.

Ensuring that a stallion stays reasonably fit after the covering season ends is neither difficult nor complicated. Running out, either by himself or with a mare or two, for long periods each day in a paddock of not less than five acres should be quite sufficient, especially if parts of it are sloped. But if the horse has only a relatively small patch of grass available, you will have to supplement the reduced amount of exercise he will give himself there with walking in hand, lungeing or riding.

Grooming is often an essential part of good stallion management. The horse that lives out all the time should not be groomed, however, since his coat must retain all its natural protection against inclement weather. Such a stallion should have his mane and tail brushed and tidied up from time to time to keep him looking as smart as possible under the circumstances.

Stallions that do not live out all the time can be separated into two types with regard to grooming: the first is groomed thoroughly while he is being readied for the covering season and during it, then is brushed over lightly each day once the breeding season has ended; the other is the horse that is kept beautifully turned out and really shining all year long. The reason for keeping a stallion looking his smartest year-round is to impress visitors, who may be prospective clients or, in the case of a Thoroughbred, perhaps shareholders in the syndicate that owns him. Such treatment is not really in the best physical interests of the horse, since it means that he has to be kept even more artificially than he would be otherwise. But it is surprising what it can do for the sale of nominations and in keeping syndicate shareholders content.

A gentle brushing over daily with a body brush once the covering season has ended is good for all stabled stallions, since it keeps them looking neat, provides a daily check on cuts, punctures, swellings, lumps and bumps and parasitic infections, and also keeps them accustomed to being handled all over. Thorough, really energetic grooming is essential once you start to get your stallion fit for the breeding season, and it should be continued until the season has ended, since it is an important aid in building a horse to his peak of fitness and keeping him there. A necessary part of stallion care is the periodic washing of his sheath with soap and water, followed by the carrying in of a palmful of olive oil and the smearing of all surfaces within the sheath.

The ideal arrangement for housing a stabled stallion is to have his loose box opening directly into a high-fenced paddock. During good weather the door into the paddock can be left open for much of the day, allowing the horse to go in and out of his box as he pleases. If you cannot have your stallion's box opening into a paddock, then try to have an adjoining runway or yard which will provide him with plenty of scope for exercise. Again, the fence of such an enclosure should be high; at least six feet for a Thoroughbred. The stallion which has the use of only a runway or yard should be turned out to graze in a suitable paddock for a minimum of two hours every day, weather permitting.

The stallion's loose box should be large; at least 18 feet square for Thoroughbreds and similar-sized horses. It should have as few projections as possible, since stallions often whirl around, and sometimes even canter, in their boxes, and should have a high ceiling, adequate ventilation without draughts and plenty of natural light. An electric light with the switch on an outside wall where the horse cannot reach it is essential, and an infra-red lamp can be useful in colder weather when a horse is unwell.

The siting of the stallion's box will mainly depend on the type and size of your stud. If you have only one stallion and a small operation without much coming and going of strange animals, you could have his box right in the main yard. The other regular inhabitants of the yard will not upset him; in fact, they will be good for the stallion, as they will provide him with the company and interest in life that he requires.

However, if you have several stallions and a much busier place, with many strange mares arriving, departing and being shifted around, you should house your stallions well away from the other stables and their occupants. Arrange the stallions' boxes so that they can look out of them companionably at each other, or, if the horses are housed in inside boxes, across the aisle at one another.

Remember, too, that wherever you site your stallion box or boxes, it or they should be fairly close to where covering takes place.

Regular attention to worming and vaccination is fundamental to proper stallion care. Just what anthelmintics you should use, and how often, and what vaccination will have to be done will depend upon the particular set of conditions prevailing on your stud. Therefore you must consult your local veterinary surgeon about them and follow his advice.

Routine hoof care is vital too, since sore feet, particularly sore hind feet, can soon make a stallion awkward at service and may even make him unenthusiastic about covering. Do without shoes when you can, and stallions living out will not need them. However, when you start working a stabled stallion to get him hard fit for the covering season he will probably need plain shoes (on his front feet at least), especially if you are walking or riding him on hard surfaces. Be careful not to let a horse's hoofs wear so much that they become painful. Conversely, if an unshod stallion is getting his exercise only on grass or a soft surface, then remember to trim his feet every month to six weeks.

Another essential facet of stallion management is the care of his teeth, which play a vital role in his life, and which, if there is something wrong with them, can have a very bad effect on his utilisation of food or his temper or both. Check your horse's teeth periodically, at least once every six months, and rasp off any developing points.

III
Methods of Management (One)

Under Range Conditions — In the Paddock All Year Round —
Inside on Winter Nights — In Shed and Yard.

The main ways in which a stallion can be managed are: roaming free
with his band of mares under range conditions; living out all year long
with mares in a paddock; staying out with mares during the warmer
weather and being stabled at night once the cold sets in; housed in an
open-fronted shed in a large yard; or kept up all the time, spending
every night of the year and a good many daylight hours of each day in
his loose box.

Just which of these systems of management will suit you best will
depend partly upon the facilities you have available in the way of land,
buildings and labour, but mainly upon your climatic conditions and
the breed of horse.

Under range conditions. This is the way that Nature intended the horse
to live and multiply, and, not surprisingly, stallions roaming free over
large areas with their mares and foals are renowned for their high
fertility, whether in the sun-baked Australian bush or on the vast pam-
pas of the Argentine.

They and their mares are kept extremely fit by the healthy, natural
life they lead, with its constant search for grass and water, and you will
find almost every mare with a foal at foot by the time that early summer
has arrived. What is more, rarely will a foal be dropped before spring,

when the natural foaling and breeding season begins, with its warmer weather, longer, lighter days and its flush of protein-rich young grass for milking mares and growing foals. If you should wish to make absolutely sure that all the foals are born during this period of optimum environmental conditions, you can turn the stallion in with the mares a month or six weeks after spring starts, and take him away from them again towards the end of summer.

As long as there is sufficient pasture and water available, and climatic conditions are not too harsh, the management of a free-ranging stallion virtually takes care of itself. You will just have to check periodically to make sure that he and his band are still around, that they have not found their way on to someone else's property through a broken fence, and that they are in good shape and healthy. Worming, feet and teeth will have to be attended to every so often; just how often will depend on your particular set of conditions.

In the paddock all year round. The practicability of this method of stallion management depends upon the climate and the breed of horse. It certainly is not for Thoroughbreds, Arabians and other finely-bred stallions in harsh climatic conditions such as those of a Northern European winter. But sleet, snow, driving rain and cold winds will not worry any of the native ponies of Britain, for instance, or well-grown, robust half-breds, as long as they have enough to eat and drink, and some shelter from the worst winds, such as a thick, high hedge.

A stallion living out all year long could spend his time outside the breeding season in the company of several mares that are in foal to him. Management at that time would simply consist of checking on him at least once a day, keeping him wormed and his feet trimmed, cleaning his water trough periodically, and moving him and his companions on to fresh grass as required.

Come winter, and you will have to feed good quality hay, ideally putting several days' supply at a time into a long hayrack in a shed in the animals' winter paddock. Such a shed, open along the front, enclosed on the other three sides and with its back to the prevailing winds, is not absolutely essential, but it is very useful, especially if the stallion is getting on in years. It is important to keep it well bedded down and clean.

You will have to keep a close check on the animals' water supply during winter, and on the coldest days you will probably have to break the ice on their trough and scoop it out at least twice a day.

To maintain condition on the animals towards winter's end (and this is of prime importance, since the stallion will soon be called upon to cover and the mares are carrying foals), it may be necessary to feed grain and/or pelleted feed ("nuts") once or twice a day. Watch out for feeding problems when the first shoots of green grass break through: often the animals will completely forsake their hay for the tasty new herbage, but, since there is not much of it in the beginning, they do not get enough to eat and quickly fall away in condition. This can be a major setback for the unprepared, especially at the end of a very hard winter. It can happen easily enough, too, since the animals' long winter coats will probably hide the first signs of lost condition from the in-experienced. However, if you are alert for this possibility and detect it starting to happen, adequate extra feeding with grain and/or "nuts" will soon put things right.

As the breeding season begins, take the in-foal mares away from the stallion and substitute a barren mare that is well in season. Cover her the first time in hand. Then keep putting barren mares in the stallion's paddock as they come into use, making sure to cover them in hand when they are first introduced to him (this is absolutely essential with maiden mares). Catch up the stallion as required to try the mares with foals at foot. He can then cover them in hand as is indicated.

Alternatively, if your stallion is gentle with foals, you could let him run with the mares and foals and cover the barren mares in hand; although I think that it is far safer to leave him with the barren mares. Under no circumstances take the big risk of mixing mares with foals and barren mares in the restricted space of the normal paddock. You will also have to be careful about crowding too many barren mares into too little space with the stallion: jealous mares may then prevent him from covering another mare by attacking him and the mare as he prepares to mount her, and under over-crowded conditions it may be difficult for him to sneak her off to a quiet corner.

Inside on winter nights. Under this system the stallion lives outside all the time with mares during the warmer weather, and is brought into his stable at night as soon as it starts to get cold. When he is spending the night in his loose box you should feed him once or twice a day, say morning and evening, and give him plenty of hay for the night hours. There should be no need for any special preparation to get him fit for covering: he will have been living a natural, exercise-filled life outside for many months before he is brought in at nights; and even when he spends the nights in a box he should be outside all day long, no matter what the weather is like. A horse kept in this way is never groomed, since he will need all the protection Nature gives him against bad weather.

This is a useful method of management for a stallion that gets some few mares booked to him but is mainly used as a teaser, particularly on a big place where there are many mares for him to try. This robust, healthy life, mainly outside with a little luxury and good food inside when the weather gets rough, the constant company of one or more mares, and the incentive of a fresh mare to cover every so often, makes for an energetic, enthusiastic and yet very tractable teaser: a big asset on any larger stud.

In shed and yard. This method employs an open-fronted shed, enclosed on the other three sides and with its back to the prevailing winds, opening into a large, high-fenced yard. A circular-shaped yard is best, since it allows the stallion to move out around its circumference freely and without having to check himself all the time as a horse in a square or rectangular yard will do.

This is a good labour-saving way of keeping a Thoroughbred or Arabian or other finely-bred stallion in a warm climate with fairly short and mild winters, and is used a lot in Thoroughbred studs in Australia's warmer areas. It is also employed on some Arabian studs in Britain during the summer months.

This system provides a very healthy life for the horse, with all the fresh air he could wish for, plenty of scope for movement and the ever-available protection of the shed when the sun scorches or a cold wind bites. The floor of the shed should be kept well bedded down, and in the warmer, drier climates to which this system is best suited, sawdust or wood shavings or even sand make an excellent bedding material.

You will need to provide the horse with green feed and some extra exercise. This can be achieved by turning him out to graze for at least two hours a day, or by cutting green feed for him several times daily, and by walking, lungeing or riding him. The amount of exercise he will require will depend, of course, on the time of the year.

IV
Methods of Management (Two)

Kept Up All the Time — Key to Success — Getting the Stallion
Fit for Covering — Walking — Long-Reining — Lungeing —
At Liberty — Riding — Stallion's Ration — A Problem Solved.

Kept up all the time. This is the way in which most Thoroughbred stallions
are managed all over the world. The key to success in this demanding
type of stallion care is an almost intuitive understanding of the horse and
his needs coupled with meticulous attention to detail, and backed by
knowledge and experience. You must get very close to the horse and
find out exactly what way of life, in all its aspects, he likes best and
therefore thrives on. Then you must go to all the trouble required to
make sure that he gets it.

And certainly few things are more deeply satisfying than producing
such a stallion at his very acme of physical fitness and fertility, a clear-
eyed, mirror-coated, muscular picture of power and animation.

Many of the basic principles of stallion care already dealt with in
Chapters I and II will have a direct application to a horse managed in
this way. Remember to cater to his need for company by allowing him
to see other horses as much as possible. They should not come too close
to him though, especially if they are strangers. Take care not to lead
strange horses, particularly strange mares, past the door of his box or the
rails of his enclosure. House him in a large, light, well-ventilated loose
box which opens into a paddock, yard or runway. Keep any such
exercise area scrupulously clean, picking up all droppings every day

when it is an acre or less in size. A sandroll measuring about twelve feet by six feet will be a useful addition to a stallion's paddock.

About ten weeks before the breeding season is due to start you can begin work to get the stallion hard fit for covering. This state of fitness can be achieved in a number of ways, all very effective, and which have their successful adherents in various parts of the world. They range all the way from walking the horse on a leading rein for miles every day to galloping him around a training track; and they include lungeing, long-reining, work at liberty in an enclosed space, riding, and combinations of walking and lungeing, and lungeing and riding. Yet, for all the variety of means, the vital end always remains the same: getting the stallion really fit for covering.

Walking is the traditional British method of getting a stallion into shape for the season, and if you have the time and labour available it can be highly effective. Always give the stallion several hours in a paddock before you walk him to get any "steam" out of his system. Alternatively, you can lunge him for fifteen to twenty minutes. He will then settle to walk much better, and instead of tending to jig-jog along on his toes looking for every excuse to play up, he will settle into the calm, rhythmic, long-striding walk that supples and strengthens every muscle of his body.

Begin the conditioning process by walking him for half an hour a day and gradually build to about one-and-a-half to two hours daily of really energetic walking, without hurry, but stepping out briskly all the time, and going up and down lots of long, gradual gradients if possible. Ideally, the stallion should be groomed thoroughly after he returns from exercise, but whether you will actually do the job then or leave it until later in the day will depend on the time and labour available.

The arrangement of a daily timetable for the horse will also be governed to some extent by his temperament and idiosyncrasies. For instance, you might ideally wish to give him at least two hours of quiet grazing in the paddock, but he may be the restless type of stallion which will cease grazing after only an hour or so outside and pace continuously back and forth in front of the paddock gate or along the fenceline. Yet another stallion, perhaps older or of a more placid temperament, might settle to graze quietly for as long as you want. There are just no hard and fast rules to follow, only basic principles which you must adapt to suit your particular set of circumstances.

When walking a stallion I think it is best to keep to the same route every day, especially if the horse is a fairly highly-strung Thoroughbred.

Stepping out over the same well-known way every day gives a horse a comfortable feeling of basic security, and allows him to relax and settle into the purposeful swinging walk that exercises him so completely; following a different route each day tends to keep him tensed up and alert for the possibility of hidden dangers in the new territory. Do not worry that the same old scenes will bore him: fresh incidents will always be occurring to stimulate his interest, from noisy tractors working in fields to curious cows trotting up to the hedgeline for a closer look at him.

I prefer to walk a stallion with a minimum of equipment: just a stallion bridle with a straight bar bit and coupling to which a well-oiled, supple leading rein is attached, and protection for his knees in the form of knee-pads. However, if your stallion has the habit of turning in towards you or biting, you should fit a rein on the off side from the bit to a roller and adjust it as required. Make sure to keep all tack well oiled and pliable, since quick, neat fitting and unbuckling of gear is essential to expert stallion handling. Slowness and awkwardness can soon bring an excited horse to the boil, and can lead to some dangerous situations for the handler.

When walking the stallion, stride out alongside his shoulder carrying the coiled end of the leading rein and a leather-covered cane in your left hand. Make sure the loop at the end of the rein is secure in your fist (never around your wrist!) so that you can keep a good hold of the horse if he should rear. The leather-covered cane is used as required to make him walk on properly and occasionally to slap him on the neck if he plays up. You must always stay wide-awake when out exercising a stallion, particularly if you are walking him on a public road (which I do not recommend), and be alert for anything which could give him a sudden fright and send him backtracking into a ditch or leaping right on to your foot!

Long-reining is really a variation of walking a stallion: the handler walks behind the horse driving him in long reins, with side reins and a crupper attached to a roller. People who use this method say that since the stallion is driven along with a fair degree of collection he is made to work all his muscles really thoroughly.

Lungeing saves time and labour but should always be combined with several hours of exercise in the paddock daily. For lungeing to be truly effective, both handler and horse must know the job properly. It is not just a question of getting the stallion to exercise himself rather hap-hazardly at the end of the long line, varying pace and the size of the circle more or less as it suits him, with the handler exerting fairly minimal control over the animal.

Instead, the handler must be able to work the stallion on the lunge calmly and correctly, making him walk, trot and canter as and when required and with the right amount of pace and extension at all times. The horse must be taught to do this, of course; not a difficult job, but certainly requiring a good knowledge of the correct technique of lungeing and plenty of previous practice with lunge rein and lungeing whip.

It is of paramount importance that the stallion be schooled to change hands quietly and without any resistance whatsoever, since a horse that baulks at reversing direction is likely to damage ligaments, tendons or muscles when he whips violently around, as he is bound to do from time to time when forced, much against his will, to turn about.

A horse that is loath to change direction is almost certainly "one-sided": he is relatively inflexible on one side of his body. When asked to lunge with the stiff side to the inside of the circle, he will feel uncomfortable at the least, and if the lungeing is overdone on that side he will begin to suffer actual physical discomfort. So if a stallion is very one-sided, most of the exercise on the lunge should initially be given while he is travelling on the hand he prefers, with short intervals only on the hand that he dislikes. These shorter periods can gradually be lengthened as the stallion becomes more supple on the relatively inflexible side, and eventually he will be able to circle with equal fluency in both directions.

Akin to lungeing is the method of working a horse at liberty in a covered school or circular yard, with the handler in the centre with lungeing whip and the horse responding to vocal commands and gestures with the whip. The advocates of this system say that a horse at liberty works with more balance and natural agility and suppleness than even the best-schooled stallion on the end of a lunge-rein, and that therefore it exercises him more effectively, in a more relaxed manner, and also decreases any risk of sprains and strains.

Riding is an excellent way of getting a horse hard fit for covering, and as well as being the most enjoyable way of accomplishing the task, will save you much time and energy, particularly if the horse is out at grass for several hours each day and you can limit exercise under saddle to a comparatively short period at more energetic paces.

Because of their very high economic value, Thoroughbred stallions of any standing should be ridden in an enclosed riding school or yard. Then, if you *should* get dumped, a huge sum of money will not go careering off across the countryside!

Exercise under saddle for Thoroughbred stallions should always be combined with several hours at liberty in the paddock daily. A good plan on larger studs is to turn the horse out to grass in the morning for at least two hours, then bring him back into his loose box for a feed just before the stallion man goes to lunch, and have him ridden after the midday break. Once the horse has been ridden, the stallion man can walk him to cool him off, then groom him thoroughly.

It is a good idea to work a horse for ten or fifteen minutes on the lunge before mounting. This initial period of exercise on the long line gives him the opportunity to get any excess "bounce" out of his system, and he can have a good-natured buck and kick at the end of the lunge without upsetting anyone.

After being mounted, the stallion should be started off at an easy trot around the sides of the school, and, after several circuits on both hands, this pace should be built into a good, long-striding, extended trot. What is required is plenty of energy and rhythm, with the horse enthusiastically on the bit, but without any rushing. He should be ridden well into the corners and not be allowed to cut them, but not be taken so far into them that he has to be checked before making the change of direction.

The best sort of rider for working a stallion in this way is not an ex-jockey crouched up on his withers, but someone who has a good basic knowledge of dressage-type riding. This is because the whole technique of riding a horse within four walls is totally different from that of exercising a racehorse in the open countryside. For a start, the frequent changes of direction within a fairly small space call for the deep, balanced seat of the dressage-type rider, plus his knowledge of the combined aids of hands and legs. Also, the more lethargic type of stallion will often have to be driven on with vigorous but skilfully-applied leg aids in order to maintain his speed and rhythm. And rhythm and balance are of vital importance when exercising a stallion in this way: smooth regularity in the work allied to vigorous but relaxed effort will have the best possible effect on the horse's musculature.

After a session of energetic trotting in both directions, the length of which will depend, of course, on the degree of fitness of the stallion, he should be brought back to a medium to slow trot to perform some school figures such as circles of various sizes, figures of eight and changes of direction across the school. This essentially gymnastic work will assist greatly in suppling and conditioning the horse if the person in the saddle really knows his job, and can accurately judge at what speed the figures should be ridden and of what size they should be for the best effect on the stallion at any particular stage. The less fit the stallion is, the slower the work should be ridden and the larger the school figures should be. As the horse becomes more supple, the trot can gradually be increased in speed, and the size of the circles and figures of eight can be reduced little by little.

Once this work has been completed, the horse should be allowed to relax and to walk several times around the perimeter of the school on a loose rein. Then the reins can be picked up again and he should be given a short session of medium-paced cantering on both hands in a fairly large circle. This short burst of faster work will have a very beneficial effect on the horse's condition as a "sharpener", but the circle should always be kept fairly large.

The workout should be finished off with some slow trotting, and, finally, walking, until the stallion has cooled down considerably and can be handed over to the stallion man to complete the cooling-off process.

On some stud farms in the United States the conditioning of Thoroughbred stallions under saddle is taken to its extreme: as well as being ridden every day, the horses are regularly worked at speed on the training track.

All other stallions besides very valuable Thoroughbreds can, of course, get their daily exercise under saddle in many other different ways: training for a show ring event; being used about the farm; or just being ridden out over the countryside. But one factor must be common to them all: the stallion must be mounted by a confident, capable and experienced rider. And while most serving stallions can be ridden in company with other horses as long as they do not come too close to them, they should never be ridden out with mares in season, other serving stallions, or, for that matter, even with colts of any degree of maturity.

The stallion's ration must gradually be stepped up in quantity as you increase the amount of work that he does, and the accent must be on transforming it into a high-protein diet supplemented with vitamins A, B_1, B_2, B_{12}, C, D and E. Feed him at least three times a day; four if you can manage it.

During the covering season the horse will require his normal daily exercise to maintain him at the high degree of fitness to which you have built him. He may, of course, get a lot of exercise then in the normal course of the day's work by being walked or ridden to try and to cover mares. Once covering starts, ensure that he gets increased amounts of protein and minerals for semen production, which makes considerable extra demands, and fresh young grass is a great help in this respect.

A major feeding problem sometimes encountered once covering begins is that a highly-strung stallion may not eat up as readily as he does in the off season and will start to drop back in condition. An extra-large feed last thing at night, when all is quiet and he has plenty of time for it with no other distractions, is often the answer to that difficulty.

V
The Basic Aim

Attainment of One End — Veterinary Opinion on the Best Time
to Cover — The Processes Leading to Conception — The Ovum
— Palpation of Follicles — Follicle Development — Spermatozoa — Fertilisation — When the Ovum is Not Fertilised —
Oestrus — When to Cover — Exceptions and Variations.

The whole complex business of stallion management is basically
directed towards the attainment of one end: the union of one of the
stallion's sperm with an ovum from the mare to give rise first to an
embryo, then to a foetus, and finally to a foal. Generally coincident
with that aim is the desire to achieve conception with the least number
of coverings; ideally, just one.

In practice, however, results often work out quite differently, with
some mares making inordinate demands upon a stallion's attentions,
and still failing to get in foal. This is where the Thoroughbred stallion
manager possibly has the edge on everyone else: he can afford, because
of the economic structure of Thoroughbred breeding, to take full
advantage of expert veterinary opinion as to when to cover a mare
with the best chance of conception taking place. The veterinary surgeon
informs himself of this by manually inspecting the state of the mare's
ovaries, of which considerably more anon.

Breeders of other types of horses, however, usually are limited to
relying on the information gained by trying the mares. And while the
external signs of ovarian activity do provide a reliable guide to the best
time for service in the majority of mares, there is always that troublesome minority of "problem" mares for which even the most conscien-

tious trying gives no guide to the optimum time for covering.

Nevertheless, even without the ever-available assistance of the veterinary surgeon to palpate follicles, the breeder of other horses is better off in one respect than the Thoroughbred man: the mares will be presented to his stallion in late spring and early summer, the natural breeding season, when they are prepared by environmental conditions to perform at the peak of their reproductive capacities.

The Thoroughbred breeder, on the other hand, must begin to attempt to get his mares in foal several months before Nature intended, and has to contend with the difficulties resulting from this artificial situation.

Before going any further, it is essential to look at the vital processes which lead to conception, and to gain a basic understanding of their "mechanics".

The ovum, which is the mare's primary contribution in the partnership which leads to new life, is produced inside a follicle in one of her two ovaries. These are suspended by the ovarian ligaments from the left and right sides of the rear part of the roof of the abdominal cavity.

The ovaries produce follicles, each of which contains an ovum, and a follicle grows in size and gradually matures until it pushes up from the surface of the ovary so that it can be felt by a person who is familiar with the technique of follicular palpation. This final stage of development of the follicle coincides with the mare's heat period.

To feel for a "ripening" follicle, the veterinary surgeon must slowly and skilfully insert his arm into the rectum of the mare, then feel through it with his fingers for a follicle projecting from one of the ovaries. Usually only one fully-developed follicle is produced at a time, but occasionally two follicles may mature at the same time, one in each ovary, or perhaps both in the same ovary. When this happens the mare should not be covered under any circumstances! If she were to be served, the almost certain and usually disastrous result would be twins.

Of course, if you are not a Thoroughbred breeder availing himself of a veterinary surgeon's skill, you will never know if a mare has developed two mature follicles at the same time. This just has to be accepted as one of the risks of breeding by the great majority, who can be comforted, however, by the realisation that twins are a fairly rare occurrence.

When the growing follicle reaches its maximum size the pressure of the fluid inside it bursts the wall and the ovum is released. This usually occurs one or two days before the end of oestrus. After being shed by the follicle, the ovum passes into the oviduct to begin its journey down to the uterus. And this, ideally, is when the sperm should be waiting at the top of the oviduct to fertilise the ovum.

The spermatozoa are produced in the two testicles of the stallion and are then stored in the epididymi, which are contained in the scrotal sac with the testicles. At covering the semen is ejaculated into the mare's genital tract; but not just into the outer region of the vagina. If the mare is properly in season, the cervix, which separates the uterus from the vagina and which is closed tight when the mare is not "in use", will have fallen to the floor of the vagina and a large amount of ejaculate from the horse will enter the uterus immediately. From there the spermatozoa swim up the oviducts towards the ovaries, and within about an hour after covering has taken place some of the many millions in the ejaculate will have reached the top of the oviduct. There they will wait for an ovum to be shed from a mature follicle.

Sperm can live, on the average, from two to four days inside the mare's genital tract. However, some very few stallions produce sperm which can survive for as long as seven days inside the mare; at the other end of the scale are those horses whose sperm will live only a day or so. Incidentally, the only way of assessing the longevity of a horse's sperm inside the mare is by practice in the field; laboratory analysis can give no assistance in this respect, although if a horse's sperm should prove in practice to be short-lived, the laboratory may well be able to explain *why* this is so.

If ovulation results in an ovum which is not fertilised, that ovum will certainly die within 24 hours (some veterinary authorities even say within eight hours) and the mare will go out of season. Another follicle in one of the ovaries will begin to mature, and will become fully developed and ready to burst and release an ovum towards the end of the mare's next heat period.

On the average, mares come into oestrus every 20 to 22 days during the natural breeding season. That is to say, there is normally a period of just on three weeks from the *beginning* of one heat period to the *beginning* of the next. The interval *between* heat periods is usually 16 to 17 days.

However, early in the breeding season for Thoroughbreds oestrus is usually weak and long-drawn-out, lasting six to eight days or more. But as the days get longer and warmer, and as the grass starts to shoot up, the heat period in a normal mare will become more intense and will shorten to five or four days or even less. In summer some mares will even be observed to be coming into season one day, will be fully in heat the next, and will be "going out fast" on the third.

Now, taking into account that the average life of a stallion's sperm is from two to four days, that a mare ovulates one or two days before the end of oestrus and that the ovum will certainly be dead within 24 hours after it has been shed, it is generally best to start covering a mare on the fourth day of oestrus early in the Thoroughbred breeding season, and on the second or third day of the heat period later on, depending on the mare. You should continue to cover her every second day after that until the end of her heat period. Usually, if you begin to cover a mare before the fourth day of oestrus in the early part of the breeding season for Thoroughbreds, or before the second or third day later on, you will just be wasting the stallion's all-important vigour. This is, of course, where many Thoroughbred breeders will have veterinary assistance in pin-pointing the best time for service.

However, these recommendations are to be taken as a very general guide only: there are many exceptions to and variations upon the normal pattern, and so it is absolutely essential for you to consider each and every mare as an individual, to study her closely, and to deal with her as her individuality demands. I cannot stress this too strongly! By all means bear the general rules in mind; but also realise that in practice you will come across a number of mares to which they just do not apply.

VI
Trying

General Principles — Trying Boards — Use of Gate or Fence for Trying — The Natural Way — The Teaser — Methods of Trying — On Thoroughbred Studs — On Other Studs — Accurate Records of Trying — Frequency of Trying — On Thoroughbred Studs — On Other Studs — The Shy Mare — The Jealous, Bossy Mare — Prolonged Oestrus — Absence of Oestrus — Foal Heat — Covering at the Foal Heat.

One of the most fundamentally important aspects of stallion management is that of trying the mares: to find out which of them are coming into season, which are in season and how strongly, and when it looks best to cover, or, in the case of Thoroughbred studs, when to get the veterinary surgeon to palpate a mare's ovaries.

Trying is also employed to find out whether a mare is holding to the stallion's service, or if she has "turned" or shows signs of doing so.

To be tried in hand, a mare is led up to a barrier, preferably a specially-built trying board but often just a gate or a post and rails fence, on the other side of which is the stallion or "teaser". The mare should be wearing a bridle if possible, since it will give the person handling her much more control.

The mare is brought up to the barrier so that she and the horse can greet each other in the natural way by touching muzzles, snorting and sniffing. Then she is led right up alongside the barrier so that she is standing very close to and parallel with it. The man holding the mare should be at the level of her shoulder, so that she will not hit him if she should react to the horse's advances by striking suddenly with a forefoot.

While the man controlling the mare keeps her in place, the one handling the entire allows the horse to work along the mare's withers and back to her hindquarters, sniffing, snorting, squealing and occasionally nipping.

If the mare is well in season she will show it by lifting her tail and twitching her clitoris (this is known as "winking" in stud jargon), and perhaps straddling her legs wide and passing urine. She may also look back at the horse and whinny softly, or lean her hindquarters or even her whole side against the barrier.

A mare that is not in season will demonstrate her unwillingness to mate by not wishing to go up to the stallion, or by not wanting to stand quietly at the barrier while he teases her, by squealing loudly and angrily, and by striking determinedly with a forefoot or even kicking out hard with both hind feet.

Mares that are coming into oestrus or which are "going off" will tend to "show" to the horse by lifting their tails somewhat and perhaps "winking", but they will also probably strike half-heartedly and squeal a little, and not seem too sure of just how they feel about things.

A Thoroughbred stud of any standing will use only specially-built trying boards for this procedure. In height such a board will come to just under the level of an average-sized mare's topline, be constructed strongly of timber and be covered on both sides with matting, have all edges rounded off and will probably have a rolling bar of about four inches in diameter along the top.

A trying board can be a fixture outside or inside a building such as a covering yard, or may be hinged so that it can be swung out of the way when trying is concluded and covering is to take place. If hinged, a board will usually have a secondary sliding head which slips securely into a socket in the floor of the covering yard. Trying boards built into paddock fences are not padded, since the animals at liberty would soon tear off the padding and possibly try to eat it.

Many studs which breed horses other than Thoroughbreds use a gate or a wooden fence for trying. This method does contain a certain element of danger, since a mare can get a leg through the bars of a gate or the rails of a fence if she strikes or kicks. However, in practice the very great majority of mares that are tried in this way know that they will hurt themselves if they shoot a leg through gate or fence, and take good care not to do so. The main risk, in fact, is to the gate, which is an expensive item, and which can soon be shattered by a determined, well-placed kick.

If I were forced to use a gate regularly for trying, I would certainly cover it with heavy-duty marine plywood on the mare's side. This will stand up to a lot of hard use and will effectively protect the gate and the animals.

But no matter how good we may be as horsemen, we cannot equal, let alone improve upon, the skill, subtlety and effectiveness with which a stallion tries a mare in Nature. Many people do not realise just how different our necessarily artificial manner of teasing mares, with a barrier separating stallion and mare and both of them under human control, is from the natural way; so it is worthwhile to take a close look at how a stallion goes about trying when left to his own devices.

Upon sighting a new or interesting-looking mare, the horse at liberty will approach her proudly from the front, neck arched, ears pricked, eyes flashing and nostrils distended. He will call loudly to her several times as he comes up to her. Mare and stallion will meet almost head on, the horse slightly off to one side of the mare's chest, just outside the trajectory of a forward-flung forefoot, and they will squeal, touch muzzles tentatively, sniff noisily and probably squeal again.

The tense stallion, standing close to and parallel with the equally rigid mare, will work his way along her neck with his muzzle, and, if she seems to be complaisant, down her withers, shoulder and side, giving an occasional short, sharp squeal and a testing nip every so often. If the mare is fully in season and is a normally demonstrative one, by this time she will have given every indication of her willingness to mate, and the stallion will waste no more time and will proceed to mount her.

However, if she is a shyer type of mare and does not "show" so easily, but nevertheless does not object to the stallion's attentions, he will proceed to work his way down her side and backwards with his muzzle until his head is twisted underneath her, and he is sniffing at and gently touching her teats. This is when even the most reticent mare, if she really is in season, will begin to lift her tail in little upward jerks and start to surrender to the powerful stimulus of the stallion's caresses. This refinement of the technique of trying is, of course, one which we cannot duplicate at the trying board.

If the mare is not really ready to mate, however, she will react with a loud, angry squeal, and by striking with a front foot. She will not actually attempt to hit the horse at first, but she will make it perfectly clear to him that she *will* strike him if he persists in his attentions. The mare may also swing her quarters over towards the horse, tail clamped down, and raise her heels threateningly in a clear indication that she will kick if he does not desist.

Now, the stallion in Nature, unlike the average horse held at the trying board and urged on by his handler, will not waste a fraction of a second more with such a mare; either he will go looking for another mate, or, if he already knows there is not one around, he will instantly lose all signs of sexual ardour, and will move away quite relaxed once again and drop his head to graze. How subtle and simple all this is, and how very different from the way we are forced to tease when mares are being covered in hand.

The closer to Nature a horse is, the better he will try, and the less time he will waste with mares that are not ready to be covered. The native pony stallions of Britain provide an excellent example of this. For instance, when a Welsh Mountain Pony stallion that is running with some mares is caught up to try a mare in hand, he will tell you almost immediately if she really is ready to be covered or not. The demeanour and actions of the mare may give the human observer every reason to think that she is ripe for mating. Yet the noisy little stallion may swiftly give a decided "No!"

A meeting of heads, some squealing and sniffing and a tentative nip or two are usually all that is needed; then the stallion will show whether it is time to cover the mare or not by continuing to squeal and snort and by "letting down", or by suddenly losing all interest in her and turning to you with an expression that plainly questions why you are wasting his time!

The further away a horse is from Nature, the worse he is as a teaser: he seems to lose that subtle sense of almost instant recognition of whether a mare is ready to be covered or not; and if he is a totally frustrated, fulltime teaser that never gets to cover a mare, he will often be far too noisy and much too violent altogether when trying.

If you have a large stud that requires a fulltime teaser, it is the best course to use a horse for this purpose that does get to cover a mare every so often. This will give him a real incentive when trying, one which will maintain his interest in this essentially frustrating task, since he will always have the hope that one of the mares is for him. It will also help to maintain his temperament on an even keel. The ideal way of keeping such a horse, in my opinion, is as I have detailed in Chapter III under the heading of *Inside on winter nights*.

On a stud of any size a good teaser is absolutely essential. You cannot use the serving stallion much for trying mares, since teasing is a demanding, tiring and mostly frustrating activity that will use up far too much of the essential energy, both nervous and physical, of a horse that has to cover a lot of mares. Of course, if you get or accept only a few mares to your stallion, you could with advantage employ him to try them, and such limited use will not affect him adversely in any way. But on bigger studs a fulltime teaser is undoubtedly necessary. He should be keen, quite noisy without being raucous, active and enthusiastic, but certainly not rough or violent, since such a teaser will only frighten the shyer sort of mare, and can possibly upset an early pregnancy when trying mares that have been covered.

As I wrote in Chapter III, the older stallion that leads a robust, healthy life, mainly outside with a little luxury and good food inside when the weather gets rough, the constant company of one or more mares, and the incentive of a fresh mare to cover every so often, will make the ideal teaser: energetic, enthusiastic and yet very tractable to handle.

This last aspect of tractability in handling is also of vital concern. Apart from the very first consideration of the danger to the man controlling the teaser, nothing is less conducive to skilful trying than an excited horse rearing half out of control from time to time, perhaps hooking his forefeet over the top of the trying board, and making such a racket and using his teeth so roughly that he does more to put a mare off, particularly if she is a highly-strung Thoroughbred, than to bring her on.

Keeping a teaser in the way that I have suggested may seem like far too much trouble and fuss to many people; actually, given the enormous contribution that a first class teaser makes to stallion stud success, this is not really so at all. With a good teaser, skilfully and knowledgeably handled, you are more than halfway along the road to that success.

There are a number of methods of trying, depending on the type of stud, the facilities available and the beliefs of the manager. On most Thoroughbred studs, for instance, the mares are tried in the morning before they are turned into the paddock. They are brought out of their boxes one after another, and taken up to the teaser at the trying board. In the case of mares with foals at foot, when each mare is led out to be tried the foal is left in the box, either alone or with a man to keep it as quiet as possible.

Other Thoroughbred studs, however, will tease the mares routinely when they come back in again in the afternoon, since the managers of such places think that teasing first thing in the morning is far from ideal. They say that the mares often tend to "tell you lies" at the trying board then, since they are impatient to get out to stretch their legs and to graze after spending all night inside. Managers who try the mares when they come back in say that after many hours in the paddock the mares are much more receptive to the teaser. But others would disagree with this viewpoint, too, claiming that the mares will be thinking only about their afternoon feed at that time of day.

Still a few other Thoroughbred stallion managers believe that it is by far the best to try the mares in the paddock about an hour after they have been turned out in the morning. They claim that this is the best way of trying Thoroughbreds because it is the method that most closely approaches Nature under the very artificial conditions of the Thoroughbred stud. After an hour outside, they say, the mares will be much more inclined to display their true sentiments to the teaser, and there will be the added advantage that they will not have to be separated from their foals, as occurs when they are tried before being turned out, and which upsets so many mares so much. What is more, in the normal relaxed atmosphere of the paddock, mares that are just beginning to come into season will often show this development far better, even though they may be standing many yards away from the teaser, than if they were taken right up to him straight from their boxes first thing in the morning.

Of course, it is the practice on many Thoroughbred studs, anyway, to try the mares without foals in the paddock. The teaser is led up to a trying board set into the paddock fence, and mares that are in season, or that are starting to come into season, will soon show their interest: they may rush straight up to the board to "talk" to him, or, even if they are shyer or are less strongly in season, will raise their heads to look, call to him, or lift their tails.

However, not many Thoroughbred studs try their mares with foals at foot in the paddock. This is because they consider the practice to be too dangerous. But the advocates of this method say that it really does not have to be risky—that it all depends on how many good men there are to assist.

To try properly in this way you need five men and yourself: one man handles the teaser; the other four go into the paddock with the mares and foals. The stallion is led up to the trying board, and, since he will have trumpeted his coming quite some distance away, mares that are really interested will already be making their way towards the board.

Two of the men in the paddock are detailed to do the actual trying: one of them catches up an interested mare, while the other secures her foal. The mare is led up to the trying board to meet the teaser; the foal is held quietly a good, safe distance in front of her and somewhat to one side. This way the mare can see the foal all the time she is at the board. The other two men in the paddock make sure that no other mares go near the mare that is being tried or her foal.

The person in charge can clearly see not only the reactions of the mare at the trying board, but also, with a little practice, will be able to spot with several sweeping glances which other mares are expressing interest in the horse, and how much.

Once the first mare has been tried sufficiently, she and her foal are led away from the teaser and released, and the next mare you wish to have a close look at and her foal are caught up.

On most studs breeding other sorts of horses, often the only personnel available to carry out trying will be one man with the stallion, who also has the added duty of checking on how strongly the mares seem to be in season, and one other person to catch up the mares one by one in the paddock and bring them up to the stallion for trial.

Or perhaps the man with the teaser will have no helpers at all, particularly if he is walking the horse routinely around the paddocks to get a general idea of which mares are in season and which give indications that they are coming into oestrus.

In the latter situation, mares that are interested in the stallion will come crowding up to the fence, touch muzzles with him, squeal, strike a little and whirl away perhaps, to come crowding back a few seconds later. It can be noisy, and often looks rather hectic and perhaps dangerous; but it is, in fact, a very effective way of trying mares, about as close to Nature as you can get with the horse in hand. And in years of trying mares under such conditions I have never known one single mare or foal to be injured in even the slightest way.

The biggest worry to anyone who is not used to the conditions on a stud where the mares are tried a lot in this fashion is that the foals are going to get mixed up in the melee and be injured. In practice it does not work out that way at all: the foals have no desire whatsoever to go anywhere near that big, noisy, menacing-looking stallion, in fact rather the reverse, and they invariably stand well back while their dams go up to greet him.

However, no matter which way you try, it is essential to keep an accurate record of the results of teasing. Best for the purpose is a large wall chart on which full information about the trying and covering of every mare can be recorded, and from which the details pertaining to each mare can be read at a glance.

On Thoroughbred studs, mares that have not been covered are

normally tried every day or every other day. Mares that have been served will also be teased every day or every second day until six weeks have elapsed from the time that they were covered without them coming into season again. After that period they can be inspected manually for pregnancy by a veterinary surgeon. If a mare has not conceived, or has "slipped", she will normally come into season again some three weeks after the start of her previous heat period. Then there are the mares which have conceived, and which stay in foal past the first three weeks, but abort or reabsorb the foetus before the 42 day stage is reached.

On other studs, mares which have not been served are routinely checked with the teaser daily or every second day. He will be walked past their paddocks, and any mares which appear to be coming into season will be caught up and tried, or, if the man with the teaser has no assistant with him at the time, at least be noted so that they can be tried later on.

Practice on these studs varies when it comes to trying the mares that have been covered. A few stud managers will try such mares on the 21st and 42nd days after service only, and make a point of watching their reactions very carefully when the teaser is around on the 15th, 28th and 31st days. Others will try the mares a number of times three and six weeks after service, and will have them caught up and tried on the 9th, 15th, 21st, 28th and 31st days as well.

However, I think that the best plan is to keep a very close check on a mare just before, during and after the period within which she would be expected to "turn", and otherwise be normally observant when the teaser is walked around the paddocks every day or two.

Therefore, I like to start trying a mare four days before the three or six weeks period from the first date of service is completed. I continue to try her every second day until four days after the three to six weeks interval from the last date of service is up.

However, when trying in this way I tease the mare only briefly: as soon as she shows the slightest sign of aversion to the horse, I have her taken away quickly, since it is possible that hard, prolonged trying at this stage can actually upset an early pregnancy. In other words, instead of subjecting the mare to several sessions of hard trying at this time, I take quick looks at her from several days before the period in which she would be due to come into heat if she were going to "turn" until several days after it is over. This span gives a very complete check, since it fully takes into account the somewhat irregular mare.

As far as in-between times are concerned, I have found that any mare which "turns out of time" will soon be obvious enough to the practised eye when the teaser goes past her enclosure on his routine tour of inspection.

Incidentally, there is one type of mare that tends to confound the novice when she is being tried three weeks after service. Brought up to the teaser, she will lift her tail, "wink", straddle her hindlegs, and perhaps give several other signs of having broken service. *However*, she will also switch her tail rather furiously from side to side all the time she is being tried. This is the giveaway; such a mare is almost invariably in foal, and should not be covered again. If you were to cover her, you would most probably upset her pregnancy.

The average normal mare will not present you with many problems in respect of trying: she will be quite obvious and straightforward about coming into season, being in oestrus, going out, and in "turning" or not. However, there are plenty of exceptions.

First, there is the mare that is shy to "show". Although, in fact, fully in season, she may not give the slightest indication that she is ready to be covered when tried at the board. But you can get a line on her true sentiments all the same. The best time to spot her real feelings is when she is in the paddock and the teaser is trying another mare; then the shy mare will often start to lift her tail and give other signs of being in oestrus, even though she may be many yards away from the horse.

Or if you house the mares in an American-style, centre aisle "barn", you can walk the teaser down the passageway to greet each mare briefly through the grille of her box. A shy mare will not "show" when the teaser salutes her, yet will begin to raise her tail and "wink" when he has moved on several boxes down the aisle. Or she may even do this before he reaches her box, ceasing to "show" as he gets close to her. A man walking well ahead of the teaser and another one following him at some distance can soon note any mare which reacts in this way.

On a Thoroughbred stud a veterinary surgeon can then examine her genital tract with a speculum and/or palpate her ovaries to decide on the best time for covering. When about to be covered, such a shy mare will often stand without "showing" until the stallion is just about to mount her, then suddenly react in the normal way to allow service to take place without any difficulty.

Another "problem" mare is the jealous, bossy sort that generally seems to have a fair dose of masculine aggressiveness towards other horses, and which often has a rather cresty neck as well. When such a mare does not have a foal at foot, she invariably develops a "crush" on another mare and will not allow any other animals near her. The jealousy of the bossy mare reaches a peak when the friend comes into season, and wants to go up to the teaser when he is making his round. Then the jealous mare will make every effort to chase her "mate" away from the horse, and to keep her as far as possible from him.

Such a bossy mare often does not "show" when she is in heat herself; however, she usually gives herself away to the really observant horseman. When she is considerably less aggressive than usual she is probably in season. Catch her up then and try her hard. At first she may squeal angrily and strike and kick. If she really plays up and is difficult to hold at the board, put a twitch on her to keep her in place and allow the stallion to tease her vigorously. Almost always she will suddenly surrender to her true desires and will "show" clearly.

But even when such a mare finally gives every indication that she is ready for mating, you should still use plenty of circumspection when covering her. And be sure to get the horse off her and right away from her heels as soon as he has completed service. A mare of this type will often stand well for covering, but will be tempted to lash out with her hind feet at the stallion soon afterwards.

Then there is the mare that stays in season for many days, even for weeks, at a time. Maiden and barren mares will often do this early in the breeding season for Thoroughbreds. This is because, at this time of the year so removed from the natural breeding season, their ovaries will not be producing eggs even though the mares are in oestrus. For this reason, studmasters often do not consider looking at maiden mares until several months after the Thoroughbred breeding season has started.

But this same problem of prolonged oestrus may occur in a mare at quite a late stage in the natural breeding season, too. Usually the mare will have a mature follicle all right, but for some reason or other will not be ovulating. Here is where the veterinary surgeon should be called to assist on all studs: by injecting the mare with Luteinising Hormone he will cause her to ovulate. Service after such treatment is often successful; other times the vet will advise you to wait until the mare comes into season again.

Other mares do just the opposite: they will not give any signs at all of coming into season. The classic case is the mare which does not come into oestrus when she has a foal at foot. From such a mare you can breed only every other year at the most. Veterinary authorities think that in a mare of this type the production of milk suppresses the oestrus cycle: when the pituitary gland produces hormones which cause milk formation it does not provide all the sex hormones which make a mare come into season.

Then there are those other troublesome mares which do not have foals at foot, but which do not show any signs of coming into heat either. The treatment generally employed with them is to "wash them out": about a pint of warm fluid, often a normal saline solution containing an antiseptic, is infused into the uterus. And fortunately this therapy often seems to work, although the veterinary surgeons are not sure why. Some think that it stimulates the cervix and that this triggers off activity in the sex glands; others suggest that it gets rid of infection which has prevented the mare from coming into season.

Trying a mare to find out when she has her "foal heat" (the first time she comes into oestrus after foaling) is a simple variation on the normal technique, dependent upon the fact that a mare will come into season from five to fourteen days after she has foaled down. A great number of mares will come into oestrus around the ninth day after foaling, but by no means all of them will do this, and so you should start trying a mare six or seven days after she has foaled, and look at her every second day at least until she comes into heat. When the mare does come into oestrus for the first time again after foaling, the foal will probably scour, and this is another good pointer to the mare's condition.

However, you must be very selective when it comes to covering mares at their foal heats: only those which have had fairly quick, normal foalings without complications of any kind, and which were not even slightly torn or bruised in the process, should be served then. And first-foaling mares should *never* be covered during the foal heat, but should be given plenty of time for their genital tracts to recover from the considerable stresses of that initial foaling.

The old idea that the foal heat was the best time of all for service has long been discredited, and many authorities now think that it is, in fact, the worst, with a low conception rate and a high risk of abortion.

VII
Covering

General Principles — Treatment After Service — Examination for Abrasions — The Lungeing Stallion — The Stallion that Bites — The "Slow" Stallion — Difficult Mares — Maiden Mares — Specifics of Service — On Thoroughbred Studs — On Other Studs — The Stallion's Book — Frequency of Covering.

The technique of covering in hand varies in its details depending on the type of stud, but the general principles governing the procedure are the same for all horses, from costly Thoroughbreds to diminutive native ponies.

The first step is to introduce the mare to the stallion over the trying board or other barrier, even though she may have been tried thoroughly by the teaser shortly before, and give them plenty of time to get acquainted. After all, this is the horse that is actually going to cover her. So allow the stallion to tease the mare properly, without any hurry, until she indicates that she is completely ready for service. Then lead her to where covering is to take place, and swiftly apply the desired restraint, such as twitch, leg strap, hobbles. If she is to wear kicking boots on her hind feet for the protection of the horse, they should have been buckled on before she was taken to the trying board.

When all is ready and the mare is properly positioned, lead the horse up behind her, not in line with her heels but several feet to her near side, and some two to three horse lengths to the rear. Check him there if necessary until he is fully drawn, then lead him forward quietly and steadily, ideally under perfect control all the way, until he is about a yard from the mare, when he can be given his head and allowed to rise up on to her.

It is important to take the horse up to the mare as soon as he is fully drawn; if you delay at this point he is likely to become too big and will not be able to insert properly, and consequently will have to dismount. This certainly interferes with the desired smooth rhythm of covering, and often upsets both horse and mare considerably.

If the mare is not wearing hobbles, it is also essential not to bring the stallion up directly behind her heels, since you can never be entirely sure that a mare will not lash out as the horse nears her. However, if she is going to kick it will usually be as he approaches her at some distance, and not in the very last moment when he is close to her and about to mount.

When the stallion rises up on to the mare, it is natural for her to move forward several steps as a result of the impact. Allow her to do this, and do not attempt to hold her rigidly in place by pushing against her, since in the great majority of cases the mare will soon stop herself and be steadied also by the grip of the horse's forelegs; then the stallion will be able to find his own position and will cover her as comfortably and as effectively as possible.

On many studs, as the horse rears up on to the mare, her tail is pulled aside to make the act of penetration easier for him. Formerly, it was often the practice, particularly with beginning stallions, to help them to insert by guiding the penis with the hand. However, modern thinking on the matter, the result of more sophisticated veterinary knowledge, is that the horse's penis should *never* be guided into the mare's vagina, since the act of handling the organ does *not* assist but only causes confusion in the chain of instinctive reflexes of the stallion at this moment. Of course, you should pay the closest attention all the time, and if the stallion should happen to thrust his penis mistakenly into the mare's rectum, he should be pulled off her immediately, since if allowed to continue he could rupture it.

If the stallion has been very active, perhaps covering two mares a day for several days running, it is as well to check that ejaculation of semen occurs by getting the man holding the horse to place his right hand gently on to the underside of the stallion's penis. When ejaculation takes place, he will feel a number of definite pulsations there. Most stallions twitch their tails upwards with each pulsation, and this distinctive "flagging" of the tail is another sign that ejaculation is taking place.

Do not drag the horse roughly off the mare as soon as he has completed service, but allow him to relax and remain on her until he withdraws and dismounts of his own accord. Keep the mare standing still, as well, and as the horse slips back off her, turn her to the left and lead her away so that she does not get any opportunity to kick out at him. Turn the stallion to the left, too, as he dismounts, and take him right away from the mare, since some stallions are also inclined to kick at the mare or the men with her after the nervous excitement of covering.

Treat the stallion immediately after service as his own individual nature requires: some highly-strung horses will need to be led around quietly for a while to get them to unwind; others can be put back into their boxes right away without any untoward effects.

Ideally, after service a stallion should be sponged thoroughly over the genitals, abdomen, chest, inside the forelegs and thighs, and anywhere else that he touches the mare, with a reliable, non-irritating disinfectant solution.

You should always make it a routine drill to examine him carefully for any abrasions, particularly of the genital organs, after service. Keep a close check on the insides of his knees, too, since horses which grip their mares tightly will sometimes rub the skin off there. Apply healing ointment as soon as you see an abrasion, since if left untreated it will only get worse, and can irritate a horse so much that it may interfere with the effectiveness of his covering.

However, horses being the individuals that they are, covering can be made considerably more difficult than the smooth operation described above by the behaviour of the stallion, the mare, or both.

First of all, there is the stallion that is impatient of control during service, although he may be perfectly amenable to discipline in every other aspect of his life. At the worst, such an impetuous horse develops into one that lunges up on to the mare from yards away, suddenly bounding forward and dragging his handler with him if the man is caught unawares. Such an unruly stallion can easily frighten a nervous mare, particularly a maiden mare, and is also likely to be kicked as he rushes forward out of control.

This disagreeable and dangerous habit can be forestalled during a stallion's early experience of covering; later on it is much more difficult to eradicate. The young stallion that objects to control during service, and which has a tendency to develop the habit of lungeing, will soon make this quite evident if you are normally observant; he must be firmly but tactfully controlled, and made to respect the will of the person controlling him.

Once a stallion has become confirmed in the lungeing habit, it will be difficult to break him of it to your entire satisfaction. He may respond for a while to increased restraint, but then, just when you think that he has settled into this pattern of improved behaviour, he will unexpectedly hurl himself forward and up on to the mare again. In this respect the confirmed lunger is rather like the confirmed jogger, and will require just as much consistently skilful handling, and the utmost concentration on your part if he is to behave satisfactorily.

The answer is not in resorting to very harsh bitting arrangements or to repeated, vicious jerking of the leading rein; this will only ruin the temper of a horse that is probably rather highly-strung and perhaps somewhat irascible anyway. Instead, it is a question of "hands", give-and-take, positioning of the mare and stallion, and the practical application of "horse sense".

Much easier of solution is the problem presented by the horse that bites his mares on the neck and withers while he is covering. This habit will obviously upset many mares, and as a result they may kick back at him, or even rear up and injure him severely. Fortunately, the various solutions are simple: you can muzzle the stallion, or you can place a driving harness collar or a rope necklace on the mare for the stallion to grip with his teeth.

Much more of a problem is the "slow" horse, the stallion which often is just not very interested in covering, and which takes a long time to achieve an erection and/or maintain one. Sometimes such horses come to the covering area much more inclined to serve after they have been warmed up by being cantered on the lunge for five or ten minutes. With others this will not work either, and the stallion's desire may need to be skilfully provoked by first taking him up to the mare as if to mount, then leading him away again, and doing this as often as necessary until he is really keen to cover.

Mares can be difficult, too, even dangerous, at covering time. Worst of all is the mare that sways her quarters from side to side; she must be kept straight and still with the help of one or more men or she may injure the horse's genital organs.

Another difficult mare to cover, especially on a small stud where there is not much labour available to assist during service, is the mare that determinedly walks forward, completely disregarding the effect of the twitch, once the stallion has mounted her. Hobbles are an obvious answer for this sort of mare, but many horsemasters, including the author, do not like to employ them for a number of reasons. One solution, if there is a good man at the mare's head, is to position her face-on to and only several yards away from a wall or fence or some other solid obstruction before the stallion mounts. Once he rises up on her, if she is kept straight by the man at her head, she will find herself right up against the barrier after only a few steps forward, and will be forced to stand for the horse.

Maiden mares must be handled with considerable skill in many cases. You must be very patient and understanding with them, and not be in too much of a hurry. There must be absolutely no doubt, of course, that a maiden mare is well and truly in season. A useful practice when a mare is being covered for the first time is to put blinkers on her: then she will not be frightened by the sight of the horse rearing up behind her. Once she knows what covering is all about, you can dispense with the blinkers.

Such, then, are the general principles of covering. Now let us look at the specifics of service, first on Thoroughbred studs, then on other types of stud.

On Thoroughbred studs. Covering on most well-equipped Thoroughbred studs takes place in a covering yard, which affords protection from inclement weather early in the breeding season for Thoroughbreds, and also allows service to take place undisturbed by extraneous sights and sounds.

A covering yard, which often doubles as a covered school into which animals are turned for exercise, will be roofed over and walled around. A good size is about 20 yards by 12 yards, and it should have excellent natural and artificial lighting. A wide door, or double doors, or even separate doors for stallion and mare of sufficient width (some five feet), will give access to this structure. Some covering yards incorporate a small mound about nine to twelve inches high: this hump is useful when a small stallion covers a tall mare, or when a big horse serves a smaller mare.

An important part of such a covering yard is the floor. Sand is excellent, since it gives the animals a good foothold and requires a minimum of upkeep. One objection to sand, however, is that in the rare case of a stallion falling just before, during or after service, it will adhere to his penis and be difficult to remove. Short-chopped wheat straw on top of sand or over a puddled clay and chalk base is also good. Another first class covering for a clay and chalk base is peat moss.

However, no matter which sort of floor is employed, it is essential to keep dust down as much as possible by dampening with water as required. Crude common salt mixed with the top layers of the bedding will assist the retention of moisture considerably. It is important to keep dust to an absolute minimum because one of the few times that potentially harmful bacteria and spores can gain direct access to a mare's uterus is at covering, when her cervix is not closed tight, as it usually is.

Four or five men are usually involved when covering takes place on a Thoroughbred stud. One of them holds the mare, one or two others assist in positioning and steadying her, one man controls the stallion, and the man in charge directs operations as well as probably pulling the mare's tail to one side.

Before being introduced over the trying board, both stallion and mare will be prepared for covering. The horse should be washed with a mild soap and warm water over the genitals, abdomen, chest, and inside the forelegs and thighs. However, when he is busy and is covering every day, or even twice a day, it is sufficient to rinse these areas with clean, warm water before service.

The mare should be washed with a mild disinfectant solution around the vulva, anus and surrounding area, and on the undersurface of the root of her tail. This whole area should then be carefully rinsed with clean water. Then a clean tail bandage should be wrapped on to her tail to keep loose hairs out of the way at service, and if felt kicking boots are to be used on the mare's hind feet (which I thoroughly recommend), they should be buckled on at this stage. If the mare has a foal, it should be left in the loose box when she is taken to the covering yard, preferably in the care of a man who will keep it as calm and as quiet as possible under the circumstances.

Then stallion and mare are taken to meet at the trying board. If the board is situated right inside the covering yard, and is of the type that can be swung out of the way against the wall, so much the better.

When the mare has been teased sufficiently, she is taken away from the board and positioned ready for the horse. A twitch should be applied, and any other restraining devices should now be put on quickly. They include a wide strap which is used to hold up one of the mare's forelegs, usually the nearside one, and various types of hobbles. Personally, I do not like any of them, since they produce too much totally unnatural restraint altogether, with a considerable possibility of upsetting a highly-strung Thoroughbred mare and of causing an accident. And, in fact, most leading Thoroughbred studs today do not use hobbles, and rarely strap up a mare's foreleg. Instead, they provide protection for the valuable stallion, which is the object of such restraint and which is absolutely essential, by using thick felt-soled kicking boots on the mare's hind feet.

If she should lash out and catch the stallion, which is a very rare occurrence anyway when the studmaster knows his job properly, kicking boots will transform a sledgehammer blow into a stinging rap. The application of the twitch will also help considerably, and in my opinion it should always be used. Further protection can be afforded to the horse, if desired, by raising the mare's head somewhat as the stallion comes up to her, as this will prevent her from kicking as easily or as hard as she would normally, or by picking up her nearside forefoot before the horse advances and releasing it as he inserts.

Once the mare is positioned, the stallion can be led up to her as described earlier and allowed to mount. As the stallion completes service, the practice on many Thoroughbred studs is for the person in charge to step in close to the mare's quarters holding a receptacle containing an appropriate disinfectant solution. As the horse withdraws, his relaxed penis is allowed to fall for a moment into this receptacle and be completely immersed in order to effect a thorough disinfection of the organ. Then he is led away and washed and examined for abrasions, as already detailed above.

On other studs. Conditions will vary considerably on these establishments, and covering may take place in a covering yard, or in a small, open yard, or perhaps just in a paddock. Normally, there will not be nearly as much labour available as on a Thoroughbred stud, and many times covering may have to be effected with only two men in attendance, one handling the stallion, the other holding the mare. However, while this minimum of handlers is often sufficient, it is always advisable to have a third person ready to assist if at all possible.

Always put a tail bandage on the mare before service, whether she is a Thoroughbred show horse being served by a small Thoroughbred in a covering yard, or a native pony mare being covered by a little stallion in the corner of a field. This will prevent tail hairs from lacerating the stallion's penis.

The matter of protection for the stallion is rather more complicated on a stud of this type, since often the mares being covered will range in size from Cleveland Bays to Welsh Mountain Ponies. Consequently, with the great variety of hoof sizes amongst the mares, you cannot provide such protection in a practical manner with kicking boots, except perhaps when the great majority of the mares are of more or less the same size.

But mares are not provided with kicking boots by Nature, either, and yet stallions running with them manage to cover without being kicked. So you will have to attempt to get as close to Nature's way as possible, with really skilful trying to determine the very best time for covering, and with first class horsemanship in the handling of stallion and mare at service.

Following general principles, try the mare, then position her, and if she is an animal of any strength or size, apply a twitch. This is sound basic insurance that should never be neglected.

The stallion should wear a proper stallion bridle, with a bit, unless he is a small native pony, in which case a strong rope halter with the lead wrapped around the lower part of his nose in a "half hitch" will often be sufficient.

Lead the stallion up to the mare, several feet to her near side, as described at the beginning of this chapter, and let the horse have his head to mount when he is about a yard away from her. An experienced stallion, before he mounts, will often reassure himself that the mare is not going to kick by bumping her quarters several times with his offside shoulder while he stays out of range of her heels.

While the man at the mare's head holds her steady with bridle and twitch, the man leading the stallion can pull the mare's tail out of the way, if desired. Or if there is a third person in attendance, he can take aside the mare's tail, unless he is needed at the mare's shoulder or side to help keep her straight or steady.

On studs where the mares come in all shapes and sizes, it will often be necessary to cover a small mare with a stallion that is considerably bigger than she is, and/or to serve a large mare with a much smaller stallion. The simple answer to such situations is a sloping piece of ground, the severity of the gradient selected depending on the relative sizes of the two animals.

If the mare is being covered in a paddock, her foal will not be separated from her. Normally, it will not attempt to go anywhere near mare and stallion while covering is taking place, and will be perfectly safe. If service is taking place in a covering yard or other relatively small enclosed space, you can put the foal into a loose box while its dam is being covered; although, since the foal may not have been handled at all and will probably become very upset when suddenly separated from its dam in this way, it is probably just as safe to have it in the covering area, where its natural instincts usually will keep it out of harm's way, and where it will have the reassuring presence of its dam. In this respect, no fixed rules can be laid down: it all depends upon your facilities, the labour available, whether the foal has been handled or not, and on the temperament of the horse, of the mare, and of the foal itself. You will have to make up your own mind about the best course to follow in the light of these various considerations.

The stallion's book. A matter of prime consideration is the number of mares that a stallion should have.

Three-year-olds entering stud can cope adequately with 15 to 20, while four-year-olds in their first season can cover from 25 to 30. Mature stallions can be given up to 45 mares each season.

It is certainly unwise to go much above these figures, since it will put too much strain on a horse and can only result in diminished fertility. As a responsible stallion manager, you should, right from the outset of a horse's career, draw up a covering programme that will give him every chance and every assistance to perform at the peak of his reproductive capacity for as long as possible. And if a stallion has too many mares booked to him, you will be faced with a very real problem when a number of them come into season at the same time, as invariably happens.

The horse may then have to cover two mares a day for two or three or even more days running, which is not in his best interests. And some of the mares will probably have to be served at a time which is not the optimum one for conception, while one or more may even go out of oestrus before they can be covered. You will, in fact, be shortchanging your horse and your clients' mares in order to get a too-large book for the stallion, and this is a disastrously short-sighted policy.

With regard to frequency of covering, it is preferable to use the horse only once a day. When he must serve two mares in one day, then spread out the covering times as much as possible.

VIII
Introduction to Stud Life

Habits Which Last a Lifetime — First Turning-Out — Letting Down Process — Trying Several Mares First — The First Service — When the Stallion is Not Successful — A Good Plan — After the First Mare: One of Two Routes — The Best Possible Base.

The habits that a stallion acquires when he first goes to stud will generally last a lifetime; therefore, it is essential at this stage to school him carefully in the best possible behaviour. Always remember that the horse's first few experiences of trying and covering will largely determine his attitude to his new role, and consequently will shape the pattern of his conduct for years to come.

Before you begin to care for the stallion, it is a good idea to talk to someone who already knows him well; in the case of a racehorse coming out of training, the "lad" who looked after him will be able to supply you with much useful information. Then, when the horse arrives at your stud, take plenty of time to get to know him as well as you can yourself.

If the new stallion is a racehorse just out of training, the first time he is turned out into the stallion paddock it is advisable, if the enclosure is a fairly small one, to station a man in each corner. Some horses recently out of training will gallop about in response to the unaccustomed freedom; if a horse does this, he can be kept going around the paddock by the men to ensure that he does not run into a corner, make any sudden, wrenching stops or slide his forelegs under the bottom rail of the fence and hurt his shins. It is also a good idea to give the

57

horse less feed than usual on the morning he is to be turned out into the paddock for the first time; then he will be much more inclined to stop running about and to get his head down to graze.

On coming out of training, the former racehorse's life will alter profoundly. He will be "let down", a gradual process which should take at least three months, during which time the large concentrate ration he formerly received will be reduced, and his hay will be increased in quantity. Instead of the fast work of the gallops, he will get his exercise in another, slower, but no less essential form. As a result of all this, his outline will change in some respects: he will lose the lean, leggy look of the highly-conditioned racehorse, and will start to round out.

His exercise should not be neglected during this "letting down" period: while he will no longer require the extreme fitness of the galloper, he must still be in hard muscular condition, if not nearly as lean, for the covering season.

Whether the beginning stallion is a Thoroughbred or a native pony, it is best to allow him to try several mares before he attempts to cover one. They must be quiet-natured and fully in season, so that they will "stand like rocks" as the novice makes his advances, and will respond to his attentions with obvious enthusiasm. These preliminary introductions to stallion life will do much for the horse's confidence if they are effected sensibly, and will also give you an idea of what to expect from him at his first service. At this stage, mares that squeal, strike and kick are most inadvisable, as they would only confuse the average young stallion, and are likely to discourage a shy and nervous one.

Allow the young horse to have ample time with these first few mares that he tries, and be patient and understanding. However, bearing in mind that these experiences are firmly setting the pattern for his all-important future behaviour, check him resolutely if he becomes too excited and impetuous, and decides that he wants to take charge. Right from the outset he must realise, without any shadow of doubt, that *you* are the one who dictates the action.

The first service given by a young stallion can range all the way from a surprisingly smooth performance to a clumsy, confusing and frustrating ordeal.

Essential to success in a stallion's first service is the mare that he covers: she must be absolutely reliable as far as temperament and manners are concerned, and fully in season, so that you can be confident that she will stand for the horse and will not attempt to kick, even if there is quite a lot of turmoil before he manages to cover her.

If such a mare is also somewhat smaller than the horse, it will be all the better.

After allowing the young stallion to try the mare at the board or other barrier, she is taken away and positioned. Then, on many Thoroughbred studs but rarely on others, a second long leading rein is attached to the coupling of the stallion's bit so that he can be guided forward and on to the mare by two men, one on each side. The idea of having a rein on each side is to keep him as straight as possible, and is an excellent one if the men in question really can work together in harmony as a team. Unfortunately, however, while this technique may sound very useful in theory, far too many times in practice the men holding the reins do *not* function together at all well, and only confuse the stallion and each other!

Anyway, whether the young horse is controlled and guided by one man or two, bring him to within two to three horse lengths of the mare and hold him there until he is fully drawn. Then take him forward towards the mare as smoothly and as quietly as possible, and *directly behind her*. This positioning, which is, of course, at variance with practice later on when the horse knows what covering is all about, is of the utmost importance at this crucial stage: if the horse does not come up immediately behind the mare and absolutely straight, he will be likely to "side mount", hooking one or both legs over the mare's back in an awkward position from which he will often have difficulty in getting down again. And while he is struggling to do so, he can easily lose his balance and fall heavily. For this reason, if you see that the horse is not going to mount the mare in the proper position, you must check him firmly, turn him around and lead him away, and begin again.

Even when the novice comes up behind the mare perfectly straight, he may still experience a certain amount of difficulty in mounting, mainly because of his ignorance of what the procedure is all about. Driven on by instinct, he will rise once or twice or more times, to perhaps half-settle on top of the mare, then get down, only to rear up again right away. You may have to pull him back somewhat to position him correctly once more, but be careful when you do this not to jerk him over backwards, which can happen easily enough if he is reared up in an almost vertical position. Any pull that has to be given then should be downwards as well as back.

As soon as the young stallion is positioned correctly, the mare's tail should be taken aside. Once the horse has managed to penetrate, he will usually complete service instinctively and without delay.

If the horse is not successful in his first attempt at service, then take him right away from the mare and walk him around quietly for a few minutes before trying again. If the stallion has not managed to cover the mare after several more attempts, it is often best to take him back to his box for a rest and to allow him to think about his new experience, then to try to cover the mare again some hours later.

Once the horse has served his first mare, put him back into his box to unwind and to rest. Make sure that he has plenty of water and hay, and leave him alone for a few hours.

If a stallion covers his first mare in the morning, it is a good plan to let him cover again in the afternoon. He will usually perform better the second time, which will boost his confidence, and this second service will be more likely to get the mare in foal, too. This is because the second ejaculate will contain many more young and active spermatozoa than the semen from the first service, which will have been stored in the stallion's epididymi for some time.

After the stallion has covered twice in the same day, you can follow one of two routes: either you can leave him for two or three days before he covers another mare, or, if more of his mares are in season, you can get him to serve a mare a day for about a week. I prefer the latter plan of action, since it provides a very effective "crash course" in covering which is the best way to confirm the young horse in the correct technique of service.

However, once the beginner has completed this rather intensive initiation, you should spread out his services as much as possible during his first season. Ideally, he should cover not more often than every second or third day. Such a carefully-managed programme will provide the young stallion with the best possible base for his future life at stud.

Stallions

Their Management and Handling

Illustration Section

1

The natural way: a Highland Pony stallion and his band of mares on the Island of Rhum. Nature designed the stallion to be a tough, fit battler, always ready to protect his mares and foals from danger, and forever prepared to fight off any other stallion that might try to take his mares away. A free-ranging stallion and his band roam over large areas seeking out their food and water, and this constant, often demanding, physical exertion means that he is in hard muscular condition all year long. And he instinctively knows the best time to cover. The high fertility of such stallions is legendary.

2

Walking is the traditional British method of getting a stallion fit for the breeding season: Epsom Derby winners Crepello and St. Paddy, and Ascot Gold Cup winner Twilight Alley, at exercise. Note the perfect positioning of the handlers, and how they are carrying the ends of the leading reins coiled neatly in their left hands. Also worthy of close attention and admiration are the magnificent physical condition of the three stallions, their faultless grooming and the spotless tack.

3

Long-reining is really a variation of walking a stallion: the handler walks behind the horse driving him in long reins, with side reins and a crupper attached to a roller. The Thoroughbred stallion Entanglement at exercise on Epsom Downs.

4

For lungeing to be truly effective as a means of exercise, both handler and horse must know the job properly. The handler must be able to work the stallion on the lunge calmly and correctly, as exemplified in this picture of Epsom Derby winner Blakeney at the National Stud, Newmarket. The stallion is flexed correctly on the inside of the circle, and is trotting smoothly around it with much impulsion. The handler's delicacy of contact with the lungeing rein is admirable.

5

Riding is an excellent way of getting a stallion hard fit for covering, and will save much time and energy, particularly if the horse is out at grass for several hours each day and exercise under saddle can be limited to a comparatively short period at more energetic paces. The splendid muscular condition, glossy coat and obvious vitality of the Arabian stallion Hassani of Fairfield bear witness to the value of this form of stallion exercise.

6

No matter what form of exercise is chosen, a stabled stallion should always be turned out in a paddock for at least two hours every day (weather permitting) wherever possible. Epsom Derby winner Mahmoud grazes in his paddock at Mr. C. V. Whitney's stud farm in the United States.

This picture shows the ideal way of housing a stabled stallion: Mahmoud's loose box opens directly into the paddock. With such an arrangement, the door into the paddock can be left open for much of the day during good weather, allowing the horse to go in and out as he pleases.

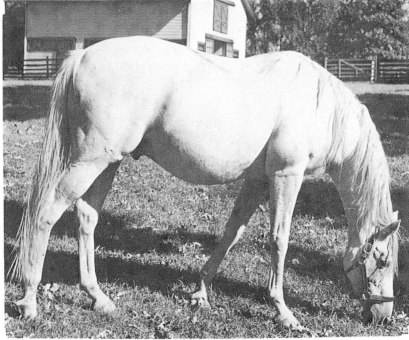

7

A happy horse: the late Mr. Henry Wynmalen's stallion Basa, who was, in the words of his owner, "kept, like an ordinary horse, in the general yard, with his top door open and able to look out and about just as much as he liked." This is an excellent arrangement on a smaller stud.

8

A mare in a receptive mood. In season, she has come up to the trying board of her own accord to greet the horse and to respond to his advances.

9

And one that is not! This mare rejects the stallion's attentions in no uncertain manner, lashing out with her hind feet and surging away from the trying board. A mare should always wear a bridle whenever possible when being tried, as it will give the person handling her much more control.

10

Kicking boots being put on the hind feet of a mare on a Thoroughbred stud prior to service. They provide excellent protection for the stallion: if the mare should happen to lash out and catch him (a rare occurrence when the studmaster knows his job properly), they will transform a sledgehammer blow into a stinging rap.

11

A mare being teased before service on a Thoroughbred stud. She is positioned correctly, close to the padded trying board and parallel with it, her handler at her shoulder out of harm's way. The trying board is hinged, and has a secondary sliding head which slips securely into a socket in the floor. When trying is concluded and covering is to take place, the board will be swung back against the wall. Note how the mare has been prepared for service: kicking boots are on her hind feet, a tail bandage will keep loose hairs out of the way, and she has been washed over as required. In this picture, the stallion handler is allowing his horse a considerable length of rein; the author's personal preference in this regard is to stand fairly close to the stallion.

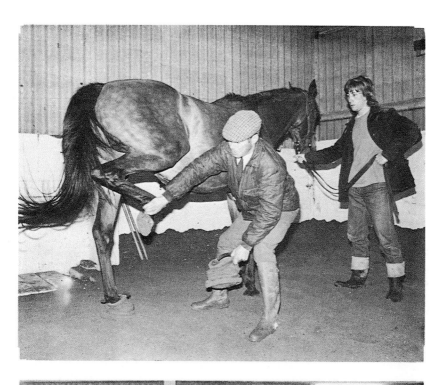

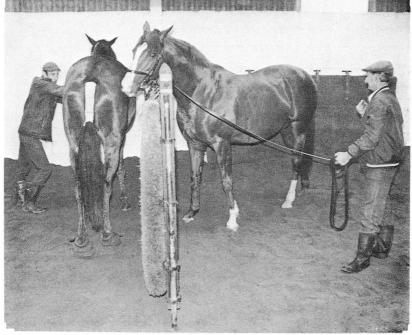

12

St. Simon: possibly the greatest racehorse and sire of all time. By Galopin out of St. Angela, St. Simon ran in ten races and won them all easily, then went on to become a powerfully prepotent sire. His trainer Matthew Dawson, who won the Epsom Derby with Thormanby, Kingcraft, Silvio, Melton, Ladas and Sir Visto, said of him, "I have trained only one smashing good horse in my life—St. Simon." Dawson also stated that, "The extraordinary thing was that St. Simon was as good at a furlong as he was at three miles, and distance never seemed to worry him." ·The stud groom at the Duke of Portland's stud at Welbeck, where St. Simon stood for so long, John Huby, said, "I always thought there was something superior, both in his action and contour, to anything I had ever noticed in any other horse."

As a stallion, St. Simon headed the list of sires of winners in England for seven consecutive years, 1890 to 1896 inclusive, and again in 1900 and 1901. Ten of his sons and daughters won seventeen English Classics, and in 1900 his progeny captured all five of the Classic races: Diamond Jubilee won the Triple Crown, Winifreda the One Thousand Guineas and La Roche the Oaks.

As an individual St. Simon was magnificent: he possessed a marvellously long, sloping shoulder, a very deep chest, and great length from hip to hock. All of this blessed with superlative quality. He also had what were once known as "galloping forelegs". St. Simon was, in fact, the very epitome of the. Thoroughbred.

13

Likeable little Hyperion (Gainsborough-Selene) was one of the most success-ful Thoroughbred sires of the Twentieth Century. He ran in thirteen races, winning nine of them and being placed three times in a three-year career. Hyperion had the speed at two years of age to win the New Stakes at Royal Ascot, then went on in 1933 to capture the Epsom Derby and the St. Leger at Doncaster. On the day that he won the Derby by four lengths he measured just 15.1½ hands high.

At stud, Hyperion was the leading sire of winners in England six times, and sired the winners of eleven English Classic races, including Derby winner Owen Tudor. Another famous son was Aureole, winner of the King George VI and Queen Elizabeth Stakes and the Coronation Cup, placed second in the Epsom Derby, and leading sire in England in 1960 and 1961. Aureole's sons include St. Paddy, winner of the Epsom Derby and a leading sire, and Saint Crespin III, victor in the Prix de l'Arc de Triomphe and also a sire of note.

14

Nearco, by Pharos out of Nogara, was bred by the Italian Federico Tesio, and was the unbeaten winner of fourteen races from five furlongs to a mile and three-quarters, including the Grand Prix de Paris. Tesio wrote of his wonder horse, "Beautifully balanced, of perfect size and great quality. Won all his fourteen races as soon as he was asked. Not a true stayer, though he won up to 3,000 metres. He won these longer races by his superb class and brilliant speed."

Carrying four crosses of St. Simon in the first five generations of his pedigree, Nearco was leading sire of winners in England twice, and was in the list of the top ten sires for fifteen consecutive years (1942–56 inclusive). He sired two Epsom Derby winners, and another two Derby winners were out of Nearco mares.

Nearco's influence in the United States has been profound, particularly through his son Nasrullah, champion sire in both England and the United States, and through Nasrullah's son Bold Ruler, leading sire in the U.S.A. from 1963 to 1969 inclusive. North American-bred Epsom Derby winners Sir Ivor, Nijinsky, Mill Reef and Roberto are all tail-male line descendants of Nearco.

15

Ribot (Tenerani-Romanella), one of the best racehorses ever and a great sire, was also bred by Federico Tesio. This superlative galloper won all sixteen of his races, including the Prix de l'Arc de Triomphe twice and the King George VI and Queen Elizabeth Stakes. St. Simon appears no less than 13 times in his pedigree.

Ribot was the leading sire in England in 1963, 1967 and 1968, and among his famous progeny are Ragusa, Molvedo, Ribocco, Ribero, Tom Rolfe, Graustark and Arts and Letters.

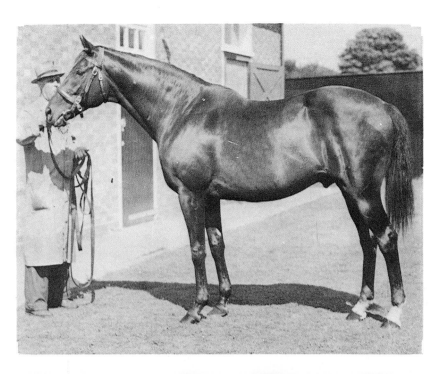

16

A feast for the eyes: the Arabian stallion Raktha (Naseem-Razina), described by the late Lady Wentworth as "magnificent, a true type of perfect Arabian."

17

The exquisite Arabian stallion Dargee (Manasseh-Myola).

18

Fantasy on four legs: the 14.2 hands high Polish-bred Arabian Skowronek (Ibrahim-Jaskolka), who founded a dynasty of stallions in England and made his influence as a sire felt in many parts of the world. He was of the classic Abbas Pasha size and type, and as well as having a superb head and neck, he possessed exceptional hindlegs and quarters.

19

Skowronek's 15.2½ hands high great-grandson Indian Magic (Raktha-Indian Crown), about whom Lady Wentworth's daughter, Lady Anne Lytton, has said, "I have always thought that Indian Magic was my mother's masterpiece, being big without losing type."

20

Quality Fair, Thoroughbred sire of hunters.

21

Anglo-Arab stallion Dancing Instructor.

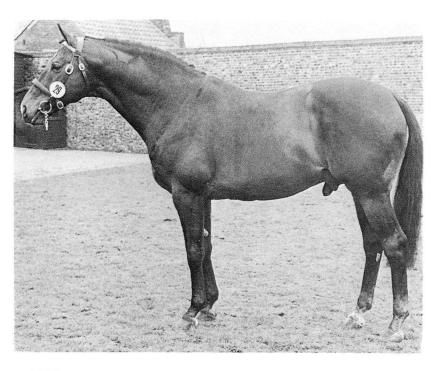

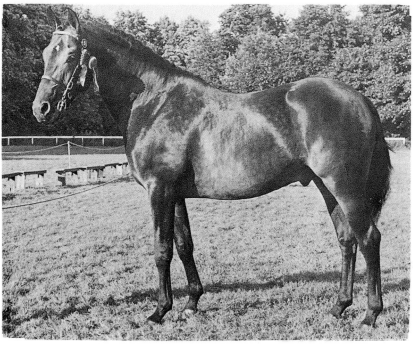

22

Palomino stallion Roundhills Golden Grenadier.

23

Cleveland Bay stallion Mulgrave Supreme, the property of H.M. the Queen.

24

The Riding Pony stallion Bwlch Valentino, who has had a potent influence on the development of the superb Riding Ponies of Britain's show rings. A blending of Thoroughbred, Arabian and Welsh, this 14.1 hands high stallion had exceptional balance and an excellent temperament, and, possessing the best of shoulders, he introduced the typical sweeping action of the modern Riding Pony.

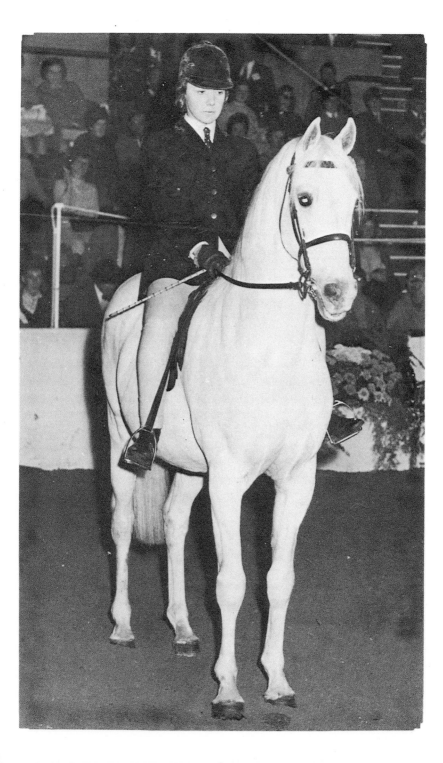

25

Bwlch Valentino's notable son, 14.1 hands high Bwlch Zephyr.

26

Quality and versatility: the small Thoroughbred stallion Ardencaple, sire of many well-known show and working ponies, hacks, hunters, combined training and event animals, and the international show jumper Trigger Hill.

27

Welsh Cob (Section D) stallion Llanarth Flying Comet.

28

The stallion Turkdean Cerdin, a Welsh Pony of Cob type (Section C).

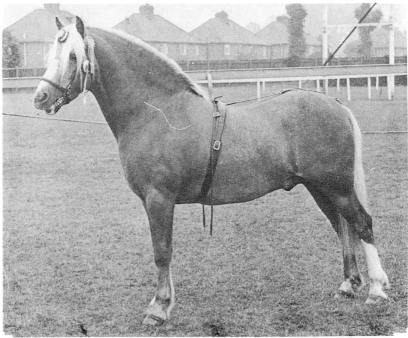

29

Welsh Mountain Pony stallion Treharne Tomboy steps out.

96

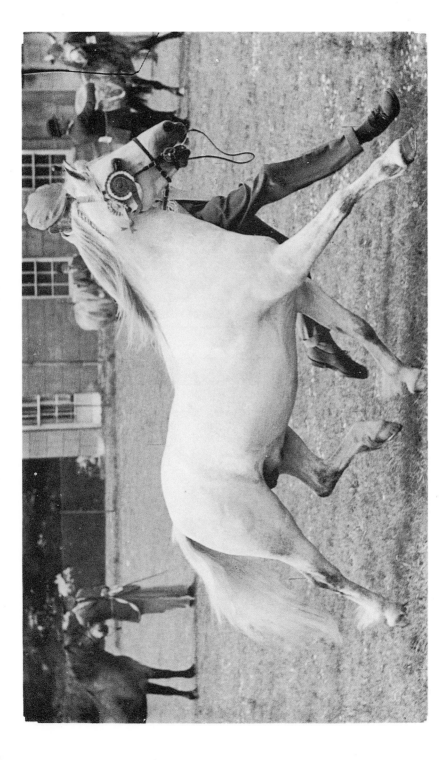

30

Section B Welsh Pony stallion Solway Master Bronze.

31

Dartmoor Pony stallion Hisley Woodcock.

32

Exmoor Pony stallion Frithsdean Peasblossom.

33

New Forest Pony stallion Peveril Pickwick.

34

Highland Pony stallion Ben Cleuch.

35

Connemara Pony stallion Leam Bobby Finn